THE NEXT TIME WE SAW PARIS

BY

SAMUEL HAZO

Wiseblood Books

CONTENTS

III. TO AIM IN SILENCE

IV. TO RUN OUT OF DESTINATIONS

V. AGAINST UNCERTAINTY

For Mary Anne,
To Sam and Dawn and their three children,
Sam, Anna and Sarah

A few of these poems were published in *Modern Age*, *Literary Matters*, *Presence* and *The Pittsburgh Post-Gazette*, but I preferred to retain the rest and not to have them pre-published in journals or other outlets so that they could be read and appreciated first in the context of this book.

ONCE

If once means once, once twice
   is impossible.
                Once is quick
   as a struck match.
                  But once
   can be a song that keeps
   singing after it's sung.
Or a poem that's once and always
   at the same time.
                To be complete
   it has to end, but once
   it's over, it begins again.

I. TO BE REMINDED

THE NEXT TIME WE SAW PARIS

"The next time was the last time."

One morning we saw de Gaulle
   himself in uniform chauffeured
   alone in an open Peugeot.
He seemed to dare assassination
   as he did near Notre-Dame
   during the Liberation parade.
On house fronts and doors we noticed
   small bronze plaques with names
   followed by *Victime de Nazis.*
We'd read reports that *Enfants
   des Boches* reached 100,000
   during the Occupation.
                                 "Horizontal
   Collaborators" were shorn bald,
   spat upon and marched naked
   through the streets.
                                 De Gaulle
   pronounced all executed traitors
   justly punished.
                                 We focused
   on Paris of the postcards: Sacré-
   Coeur and the Eiffel Tower.
The Folies-Bergère booked sellouts.
The Bateau Mouches was packed.
Lounging by the Seine, a fisherman
   propped his rod against

a bench and smoked a Gitanes
as if catching a fish meant
little or nothing at all.

NIGHT IN THE EYE OF THE SUN

In La Napoule with Mary Anne
   I order mussels steamed
   with aioli, two cappuccinos
   and a warm baguette with butter.
It's almost dusk in La Napoule.
Two waiters are laughing in French
   and folding serviettes.
                We talk
   of Avignon and Aix-en-Provence
   where thousands of sunflowers
   follow the sun to sleep,
   and aisles of lavender look
   truer than they are.
              We say
   if colors can intoxicate, these do
   and then some.
            It's darkening
in La Napoule.
           We dine
   like partners who have earned
   the ease that work makes possible
   and doubly bountiful because
   it's earned.
           Throughout America,
   where ease means laziness,
   that art is lost.
           In La Napoule
   the night is ours to waste

creatively.
          The buttered crust
of our baguette tastes almost
like the eucharist.
          Tomorrow, fireworks
will celebrate the fall of the Bastille
before the coast grows calm
again.
          The docked and anchored
yachts will mute their lights.
Beach-crews will stack the sunning
mats like so much stock.
The sea that hides more history
than all the oceans in the world
will slow its tides.
          But that
is still a sun away.
          Our private
table feels so much like home
that we forget the time.
It's midnight now in La Napoule.

WHAT SEEMS, WHAT IS

Not that it matters…
                    Skyscrapers
  in Hudson Yards may dwarf
  the desert towers in the emirates.
So what?
              All those who batten
  on irrelevance can feast on that.
Let rocketeers re-name the moon,
  establish malls on Mars
  and conjure floating cities
  in the sky.
              What difference
  will it make to killers in uniform
  who boast of bombs that prophesy
  extinction?
                If soldiery's the norm,
  then wartime killing will stay
  the alibi for murder.
                    It seems
  unending.
              As one who thinks
  that love in all its bravery
  can mock the follies of this world,
  I see how disappearance
  lets the unforgettable endure.
What lasts recalls what's lost…
My wife's smile was love
  and bravery combined.

It made
our kind's unkindness something
to defy.
The world is less
without her.
And so am I.

VIGIL

Darkness is illiterate.

                You
wait for a word, but there's
nothing.

           You wait for a sound,
and there's nothing.

              Midnight's
a time of its own.

             Whatever
it hides is yours to imagine.
You almost hear a voice
you loved above all others.
You'll hear it in your dreams.
But now there's only midnight
and silence.

          You close your eyes
and keep them closed, and listen.

THE EYES OF LOVERS

They'll look at each other
   until whatever prompts them
   to keep staring surrenders.
They'll learn that all they ever
   hope to see stays near
   as here but hiding.
               Their eyes
   will fence to a final draw
   that neither even wants
   to win.
        They'll think no more
   of elsewhere or yesterday
   or anything ahead to interrupt
   the marriage of their eyes, mating.

WHEN ONE IS THE PLURAL OF TWO

I

With side-saddling outdated,
   she's post-Victorian.
               She stirrups
   her boots and straddles the saddle.
Off at a gallop, she crouches
   and shortens the reins until
   she and her horse seem one
   and the same.
            It's not for show
   since what she gains in notice
   she loses in grace.
            Result?
A union of talent and action—
   the one perfection we can earn.
It's what can happen when,
   singing, we become the song.
Or when asleep we're suddenly
   awakened from a dream so
   intimate and true that we
   confront the dying world
   like rebels.
          Or least imperfectly
   when love and loving keep us
   nearer and closer and one.

II

What counted for some was numbers.
Mad Jack Donne had mistress
   after mistress before he woke
   and married Margaret.
                   Don
   Juan lost count.
             Casanova
   forgot each woman's name.
Lord Byron scorned his fellow
   poets, swam the Dardanelles
   and proudly philandered at will.
Simenon relieved his boredom
   by playing with a new pair
   of breasts.
           For Romeo and Juliet
   and all who love as they
   loved, who bothers to play
   with numbers?
           One plus one
   is never more than one.

MASCULINE, FEMININE

Men do whatever men
    can do, and that's that.
Later they wonder how
    and why they did it.
                Questions
    arise.
        Being men, they cope.
They make amends.
              Outliving
    their private hells of downs
    and ups, they come to be
    impersonal as nouns…
                Being
    verbs by nature, women
    mock such pantomime.
              For them
    redemption through remorse
    is wiser than regret.
            That's why
    they always seem in action
    even when they rest or sleep.
Paired as a species with men
    like parts of speech, the verbs
    remember what the nouns forget.

CONJUGALS

Each one is the other's only
    other, and so they mate
    without impatience or pretension.
Kisses are their secret language.
Their differences reject what
    difference means whenever
    they embrace.
                  They have the gift
    of making imperfections perfect,
    and thoughts of death ignorable.
Parted by necessity or fate,
    they'd feel like amputees.
The fear of that returns them
    to themselves.
                Nothing
    must come between them.
And nothing can or will
    undo their perfect fit.
Together they complete each other
    solely for the need of it.

Sentenced to Survival

The future never happened,
    and the time that should have
    happened vanished on arrival.
The clocks ran backward.
The days were more like nights,
    and the nights were endless.
One life from two was over.
Your days of working, shopping
    for one and waking alone
    returned.
            You came to see
that a life unshared made
living a struggle.
            Dealing
with the curse of dreams recalled
her voice, her touch and all
your ways together.
            Your gratitude
for times you'd suddenly remember
eased the pain but only when
they came without coercion
or remorse.
            Forcing them
back made everything worse.

A LOVE LIKE NO OTHER

It happens rarely, if at all.
Age means little.
                History
        means less.
                        All that matters
        is the mystery.
                        From infancy
        to manhood our son's love
        for his godmother never lessened.
Sixty years between them
        made no difference.
                                For hours
        they could sit in the same room,
        say little or nothing and be
        perfectly happy.
                        Once
        she even let him cut
        her hair…
                        A decade later
        she told my wife during
        their last moments together,
        "A very nice young man
        always comes to see me,
        and he looks just like your son."

GIFTED AT CHRISTMAS

Yesterday morning I ate
   breakfast alone in a restaurant.
A little girl at the next table
   with her grandfather smiled
   at me.
        I smiled back.
                   Then
   she ran to my table and placed
   a cellophaned candy cane
   in my hand and said, "For you."
I'm thinking of her now.
It's four in the morning.
               Except
   for a slowly passing car—
   no traffic.
        Out of the night,
   a siren…
         At home alone
   in the dark, I trip on a rug
   below a portrait of my wife.
I blame and damn the rug…
Suddenly a child's smile
   brightens everything around me.
I wonder how she found me.

To Amira Willighagen

I listen to a nine-year-old
   Dutch girl singing Puccini
   on stage alone as flawlessly
   as Callas or Netrebko.
Her voice halts me.
              I want
   to word my feelings, but nothing
   happens.
           I have words in surplus
   for the virus-ridden air,
   for cities gone to chaos,
   for soldiers trained for homicide
   in chosen wars.
            But now
I'm wordless.
           Hearing a child
sing *mio babbino caro*
evokes from women and some men
intelligent tears.
           Applause
seems insufficient.
           No one
speaks.
        Like lovers who talk
after or before but never
during, they keep to themselves
the ache of love, happening.

LIFE AT A DISTANCE

We've all been self-imprisoned
    for a week and warned of worse
    to come.
             Robins, finches
    and sparrows peck and perch.
It's sunny but chilly today.
It's pretending to be Spring.
We number six hundred
    Pennsylvanians less than yesterday.
It's even worse in Michigan.
The whole country's a target.
To date there's no defense.
My neighbor's wife stands
    alone on her back porch
    with her dog.
             She waves.

                    I wave.

II. TO LIE IN WAIT

SAVED FROM THE SEA

Choppy or calm, the sea
    bothers me.
           It always seems
    to be lying in wait.
             Always.
Before I was six, I fell
    unseen from a dock and was saved
    from drowning by a stranger.
That moment comes to me
    in dreams—the sinking, the saving.
Now I swim well enough
    to save myself, but doubts
    still bother me.
           I never
    relax in the water.
           Never.
Even when I've dared myself
    to swim farther than I should
    and back, the sea still wins.
It never loses.
           It never
    will.
           It never can.

INBRED

Finches arrive in bunches.
They helicopter down and hover
    like hummingbirds before
    they peck in order at the feeder—
    each to his ration.
                No one
fights.
        A wild but definite
    civility prevails until
    each finch is full.
              To share
    and share alike is worlds
    away from all our public
    massacres or wars we wage
    for warfare's sake.
              It seems
    we are the lone species
    that kills its kind by choice.
Lately we've invaded space
    and set our sights on Mars.
Will we retain our malice
    in the stratosphere and be
    as lethal there as here?
              The first
    murder on the moon will tell us.

GENESIS

Spurning the fairy tale
    of Eve and Adam, some claim
    we started as one before
    we split in two.
                If true,
    the split explains what draws us,
    each to each, to be complete.
We're creatures born with groins—
    or loins, if you prefer.
                We keep
    them fig-leafed out of modesty,
    as if ashamed.
           It takes
    an artist to reveal what stays
    concealed so we can see
    how perfectly compatible we are.
Medical charts confirm
    we fork alike below
    our equatorial waists.
We're quick to note the difference.
One has what the other lacks.
One lacks what the other has.
Conceivers persist.
           Receivers
    assist.
        And the split goes on.

ALL AT ONCE

The once of close calls
in St. Tropez and Saranac—
the once of Kakie's room
with everything in order
down to hairpins—the once
of being told to think
of dying as the "death process"—
the once (if you're lucky or picked)
of knowing that love outlives
both lover and beloved—the once
of a marshmallow swallowed warm—
the once of watching your son
conduct an orchestra—the once
of waiting and waiting and waiting—
the once of seeing that greed
means more than enough
while saving is greed reversed—
the once of baseball or Shakespeare
where time's ignored, and all
that matters is performance—the once
of saying that sin means harming
someone on purpose, including
yourself—the once of wanting
what happened once to happen
once more or never again.

A PICTURE'S WORTH A THOUSAND

Before photography, everything
    was hearsay, transmitted
    by script or printed.
                  Cameras
    changed all that.
              Photographers
    became snapshot historians,
    and photographs denied denial.
Capa's photos on D-Day
    recalled what Brady filmed
    at Gettysburg.
           For Duane Michals
    and Helmut Newton, a female
    nude who spurned the shame
    of clothes was naked by choice.
Cartier-Bresson preserved
    what others overlooked.
                Leni
Riefenstahl made cinematic
    art of Germany's Olympics…
We'd be a different people
    if cameras existed twenty
    centuries ago.
           We still would
    say a Nazarene was crucified.
But who could deny a miracle
    if he was photographed a week
    later risen and walking

with friends to Emmaus?

                        The name
of Paradise Lost would change
to Paradise Found.

                  For all
but blind believers, sight
and belief would be the same.

When Being Rude Seems Right

Whenever he says, "I'm really
　　twenty-five, not twenty-six,
　　because I was sick for a year,"
we smile.
　　　　　That's just his way.
If he meets someone who says,
　　"How do you do," he answers,
　　"Do what?"
　　　　　Whether asked
or not, he claims, "No one
　　visits a rest room to rest."
Unfazed by football millionaires,
　　he murmurs, "Boy-men at play
　　for pay."
　　　　　Regarding fashion?
"Burlesque with a price tag."
His opinion of beards?
　　　　　　"They hide
　　the face."
　　　　Of stubble?
　　　　　　"Someone
　　too lazy to shave."
　　　　　Of tattoos?
"Skin-deep doodles."
　　　　　On modern
　　poetry?
　　　　"Sociology in stanzas."
Mocked and dismissed because

he offends, he says, "Each day
we're here to be offended."
His thoughts on war?

                    "Everyone
loses."

       And peace?

             "Really?"
And life?

       "It's what we're missing."

THE SERVITUDE

"The pen is a second tongue."

I

Poems come all at once
   or in stages.
            Jealous as love,
   they leave no room for distraction.
A forced poem mimics
   a forced marriage.
              Failure
   is only a matter of time.
Interrupted, a poem returns
   beyond denial like a love
   that's chosen, conjugal
   and undeniable.
            Similarities
   are obvious even when
   they seem farfetched.
            Asked
   if he believed in God and why,
   one widower said, "I want
   to see my wife again."

II

To remember wherever you were
   whenever you said whatever
   was heard by whoever was
   with you is just a distraction.

Why do you think there's a past
    to remember?
                    Time past is still
    present.
                Time present is passing.
Time future will pass.
                    You fret
    like poets who suffer to say
    what they alone can say.
You wait for that moment to come
    the way a male cardinal waits
    for his mate, and she finds him.

WHO?

Recogniton's not the problem,
  but craving recognition is.
Some bet on how they look,
  but banking on looks is fickle.
Consider movie stars long past
  their prime and unremembered.
The same holds true for those
  who make what's private public
  merely for attention.
                      When something
  singular in private becomes
  plural in public, it loses
  all distinction.
                  Distinction is what
  all wire-walkers, astronauts,
  strippers and assassins want.
                          Assassins?
Every President's assassin
  but one wanted to be known
  for what he did.
                  Oswald
  was blamed for doing what
  was done and then denying that
  he'd done it.
                  Murdered before trial,
  he'll always be guilty as charged
  for what he never admitted.
Lone gunman, lone liar or lone
  patsy   he changed a century.

The United *Status* of America

Smoking my pipe, I offered
 Halloween candy to a boy
 who focused on the pipe and asked,
 "What's that?"
      Next—a wedding
 where the bride had the date
 of her marriage tattooed
 on the back of her neck.
      Then—
newscasts ranging from alarm
to charm.
     Then—cars equipped
to drive, stop, turn and park
themselves.
     Then—round-trips
to the moon for three million per.
Then—tracing ancestries back
 to Adam or part way.
      Then—
students who print their names
because they never were taught
to write them.
     Then—a third
grader who said that poetry
means "putting your best words
together with feeling in them."
That made up for everything.

SEE HERE

From right honorables to royal
   highnesses we recognize
   their names.
          Ruling by right
   of vote or sperm, they smile
   and wave.
          Whether we need them
   or they need us means little
   to us and less to them,
   and nothing to the world.
               Ice
   in the Arctic continues to shatter
   and melt.
         Nuclear bombs
   stay poised for launch to vaporize
   Boston, New York and half
   of Russia in minutes…
             Between
   the status quo and Armageddon
   we numb ourselves with spam.
Retirement buyouts promise
   time to travel and loaf.
Vitamins are guaranteed to lengthen
   life equated with arithmetic.
Capsules and plastic surgery
   offer instant adolescence.
Finally, we learn that all
   we have is what is ours

to give.

               Was this what prompted
Mickey to make her cottage
a work of art?

                     Or why
Mary Anne chose the perfect
godmother for Sam?

                     Or how
Edison saw darkness as the enemy
of light and did something about it?

DESIRE

The French call it an excess
   of health.
          Dante named it
   a beast within us.
             St. Francis
   blamed it on Brother Ass.
Seen as a surplus, a carnivore
   or beast of burden slanders
   desire as just another
   appetite.
          Aristotle claimed
   it could be tamed by moderation.
Mystics and ascetics chose
   denial as the only answer…
After it survives denial,
   it keeps us savage in war,
   suspicious of peace, exultant
   in love, impatient when ill
   but always determined.
             Energy
   becomes its synonym—with death
   its contradiction.
           It wearies us
   with deeds and freshens us
   with sleep.
         It lets us rise
   redeemable or damnable,

murderous or generous,
uplifting or disgusting
merely by letting us be.

WORLDS APART

An American billionaire donates
   a miniature sub and flies
   expert engineers to Thailand
   to offer free expertise.
Divers from multiple nations
   volunteer their services
   to save twelve boys and their
   soccer coach trapped
   in a flooded cave for weeks.
Knowing their lives could be
   at risk, they dive regardless.
One dies, but the boys and coach
   are saved…

                    Elsewhere?

                         Mothers
   stranded in Texas or Mexico
   weep for children sundered
   and lost—assassins gun down
   concert goers or third graders
   with weapons of war—hundreds
   of refugees in flight from Libya
   drown near Sicily—Trumpism
   trumps Trump—Israeli
   snipers near Gaza target
   three unarmed boys
   protesting at the border, killing
   all three, their catch for the day.

Thou Shalt Kill

On D-Day alone ten thousand
  died.
      Cemeteries in France
commemorate them, grave
by grave…
        The battle of Tarawa
lasted for seventy-two
hours.
     One thousand
marines were killed or drowned.
Their bodies floated face down
  in the tide or sprawled half-buried
  in the sand.
       Of four thousand
eight hundred Japanese,
only seventeen survived…
Nations rightly honor
  the lost.
     But killing is killing.
When waged for honor and other
  deceits, war makes the killing
  likelier and lawful.
       Historians
claim that Greece made war
on Troy over a kidnapped wife
named Helen.
      In fact, Helen
welcomed the abduction.

                              Paris

was young and handsome compared
with the braggart she married.

                              Greeks

would fight to save a kidnapped
wife but not one who loved
her abductor.

              They settled instead

for a plausible lie.

              Determined

to trade on the Black Sea
that Troy controlled, the Greeks
knew war was the key but only
if seen as noble.

              Rescuing

Helen of Troy from Troy
is what their cause became…
When dangers widen into wars,
   what worked at Troy still works
   though Troy is off the map,
   and Helen has other names.

                    To Stuart Herrington

III. TO AIM IN SILENCE

Shoe Horn

It has the curvature that eases
   ankles into heels until
   each foot feels fitted and shod.
It looks plainer than a spoon,
   but it works.

               It always works.
It could have been what kept
   Samson from limping shoeless
   in Gaza, or Richard from screaming,
   "My shoes, my shoes—a kingdom
   for my shoes," or Babe Ruth
   from circling the bases in socks.
Excuse the play on words…
But serious trivia may not
   be as significant as thought
   when flanked with deeper issues.
Brutus was illegitimate.

               Caesar
   was in fact his father.

               Roman
   families of status conversed
   in Greek.

          When Shakespeare's Caesar
   utters, *"Et tu, Brute,"*
   just before his son stabs him,
   he should have said it in demotic
   Greek, not vocative Latin.

MAPLEDOM

Their branches beckon like the arms
    of ballerinas.
                From May to October
    their leaves brighten from burgundy
    to orange to tan.
                In the newsworthy
    world of havoc and other
    distractions, maples create
    no headlines.
                Although they've sieved
    the wind through fifty years
    of war after war where millions
    died for nothing, they tell
    no time except their own.
Here in the land of Oz where
    total extinction is likely,
    the maples offer no defense
    but nonchalant irrelevance.

CHIPMUNKIAN

I

He follows his nose to anything
   that smells edible.
                  He squats
   like a catcher, clutches a nut
   and munches.
              When he tunnels,
   he tunnels for one.
             Never
   wasting a step, he knows
   exactly what's ahead,
   behind, above.
            With cheeks
   plumped or slack, he shows
   how cheeks can store the not
   yet munched.
           Why ask if chipmunks
   serve a purpose other
   than the perfect way
   they munch and store?
           At least
   they prove perfection at ground
   level or below is possible.

II

Seeing a single chipmunk
   dead, fat or asleep is rare.

They have no time for such.
Right now or what's next
   is all they know.
                    Compact
   as a change-purse, they nose
   the ground, glance up, dart left,
   skitter or flex erect.
Dinosaurs have gone to extinction.
Hippos are soon to follow.
Chipmunks foretell how
   the meek shall inherit the earth.

BACKYARD ZOO

Twin foxes today, not quite
    as red as expected, but foxes
    for certain…
                Yesterday a possum
    walked the window ledge,
    leaving paw prints on the glass…
Otherwise the usual: white-tailed
    fawns or young does tripping
    like ballerinas in the grass,
    a male wild turkey splaying
    tail feathers in a fan, groundhogs
    and chipmunks in open stealth,
    a pheasant parading like a king
    with seven queens, a skunk
    protected by the private threat
    of stench, a turtle mimicking
    a soldier's helmet on legs
    and plodding east southeast.
My backyard's home to all.
Roofed from birth, the turtle
    disagrees.
            He has no truer
    home to seek than where
    he is no matter where
    he is or where he goes.
If he gets there, he gets there.
If not, he's there already.

Trees are a Parable

Even the misshapen retain
    a definite grace.
                Although
    it took decades, a sprouting
    tree in Malahide U-turned
    back into the earth, surfaced
    and grew sideways.
                Willows
    in the wind resemble ballerinas.
Cypresses spire at permanent
    attention.
            However briefly
    magnolias bloom, they're worth
    the wait.
            Oaks, maples, poplars
    and elms obey their calendars.
Cedars that survive in Lebanon
    still glorify the mountains
    of the Lord.
            Thickening, ring
    by ring, from a pinpoint center
    in their trunks is how trees reach
    randomly outward and upward
    and aim in silence at the stars.

STEPS AND STONES

Her black hair is cut short
   and parted on the right.
                       She's
   dancing near the Parthenon
   with two men on either side
   of her, their hands aligned
   on one another's shoulders.
Her feet are speaking fluently
   in Greek.
             Bouzoukis match
   her every step…
             In fact,
   she's dancing on what's left
   of the Acropolis—a cemetery
   now of crumbled stones
   that sleep with history and other
   lies.
         Concluding the sirtaki,
   the dancers smile and wave.
The stones foreshadow oldness
   without end.
             The dancers
   disagree.
        They make their own
   tempo, and there's no debris.

BEHIND WHAT'S AHEAD

Ahead becomes behind
too quickly to be understood
except backwards but only
partially and even then
so colored by confusion
that months or years might pass
before the first inklings
of insight tell you that what
you saw or heard was not
what it appeared to be
but something totally different
and at odds with memory itself
like all the altered views
of Kennedy's death from murder
by a lone assassin to covert
execution, theories of Amelia
Earhart's fate, verdicts
on Pacelli's papacy or almost
anything that passes for history
since history is what was thought
to have occurred by those
anointed by themselves to say so
exactly as I'm doing now
for no one's benefit but mine
because my views are no
more credible than those of anyone
who must at last conceed

that what was once ahead
for not that long would stay
both inconclusive and confusing.

VENGEANCE

Married and titled as Lady
    Caroline Lamb, she was twice
    a mother.
               Byron was Lord
    Byron whose hobby was women.
"Mad, bad and dangerous to know,"
    she said of him.
               "No love
    could be outdone," she added,
    "like one that's felt for the first
    time."
            Their bond was poetry
    and passion.
            To meet him
    in secret she dressed as a boy
    or wore a mask.
             Knowing
    he was clubfooted, she flirted
    and danced with total strangers
    while he watched.
                 Not once but twice
    she fought him with a knife before
    she was subdued.
             Repeated
    spats defined them as a pair.
After they spat their last,
    she mailed what she believed
    was all he understood of love—
    two snippets of her pubic hair.

Weddings These Days

I

The bride came to church on a tractor.
The groom and groomsmen
  were filmed helping her board.
The tractor itself resembled
  a semi-tank on treads.
The groom did all the driving
  while his bride sat beside him
  and frowned.
                What everybody
  would always remember
  would be farm machinery driven
  by a groom with more nerve
  than taste.
              The bride never smiled.
Dressed in virginal white
  and wielding a bouquet (since this
  was, after all, *her* wedding), she thought
  this whole charade would vanish
  if she just sat still...
              It stayed.

II

One bride at her wedding chomped on
  loud bubble gum while flouncing
  down the aisle.
            At another,
  the groom wore high-laced

yellow sneakers.
                              At a third,
the bride dallied for an hour
outside the church because
she wanted to be sure.
                              At a fourth
were two who took each other
for better or worse while skydiving
down to Texas.
                              Another two
exchanged self-written vows
with sign language side by side
in divers' apparatus underwater.
The sixth and last was a home
    wedding where the groom,
    having fainted twice, was married
    seated and awake but incoherent.

VERDICT

You wait for politics to wipe
   its nose and wash its hands
   of him, but nothing happens.
You look for help from history.
Then you remember how
   a predecessor won every state
   but one before resigning
   in disgrace.
               Had he won
   Massachusetts, Richard Nixon
   and George Washington would be
   paired in unanimity forever.
You're left to read the dice
   of democracy's crapshoot.
Oratory died with Kennedy.
While defecating, Johnson met
   with Secretaries of State
   and Defense.
             Ronald Reagan
   brought Hollywood to Washington.
The lesser Bush excelled
   in cheerleading.
               No one but Obama
   chose targets for the drones.
Trump's favorite presidential
   color?
       Sunlamp tan.

OUT OF THE BLUE

For years I knew of only
 three Sam Hazo's—my father,
 my son and me.
      Last year
 my son received an email
 signed Yvonne—from Toulouse.
It was, in a word, affectionate.
He called and asked discreetly
 if I knew an Yvonne in Toulouse.
My answer was a discreet
 but curious no.
      He began
 searching by name and found
 a certain "Hazo, Sam" employed
 by Airbus in Toulouse.
      Rather
 than answer or forward the email,
 he scoured further and found
 throughout France forty-seven
 similar Hazo's.
     Instead of telling
 Yvonne of all these options,
 he thought it best to mention
 only Airbus Sam and let
 the other forty-seven Hazo's
 find their own Yvonnes.

DANCERS

"Prose is to poetry what walking is to dancing."
—Paul Valery

Belly-dancing has more lure
  than grace.
            Jansenized north
of the waist, Irish step-dancers
show that legs have minds
of their own.
          Even if
they try, no couple can look
unhappy or bored while dancing
a polka…
          When Fred Astaire
united tap and ballet
on the ballroom floor, all
we had to do was watch
and listen, and the dancing did
the rest.
          The weightless grace
of every step identified
a generation: Gene Kelly,
James Cagney, Ginger
Rogers, Eleanor Powell
and Cyd Charisse.
              Each one
has danced and gone.

                            All
that survives is what they left
on film.
                    We watch and listen.

Salutes

To Marilyn, who dedicated her novel
  to her husband and their sons—
  "four wonderful boys."
To Greg, who thanked his directors
  and fellow actors for their praise,
  then turned to his wife and said,
  "Veronique, you're the only girl
  for me—I'll see you later."
To Oscar, who barked a whimper
  and looked his last at me
  before the vet injected.
To Julia, who returned the applause
  of four thousand in the audience
  with a smile, a bow and a wave.
To Sam, who accepted as conductor
  the orchestra's orchid bouquet,
  then walked to where his mother
  was sitting and presented it to her.
To the Marine colonel, who agreed
  when I called the wars in Vietnam
  and Baghdad presidential crimes.
To Kennedy, who spoke in Dublin
  of the fallen boys of Wexford
  with Eamon de Valera watching.
To the woman with a Polish accent,
  who gave me road directions

and said, "You made my day"
when I thanked her in Polish.

To Wanda DeSimone

IV. TO RUN OUT OF DESTINATIONS

THE PAINTERS OF NUDES

Like girls not yet aware
   of what a woman's body
   means, they offered Renoir
   the texture of skin.
                  On canvas
   they became an old man's dream
   of women playfully nude
   for him alone…
                Picasso's
   early nudes look almost
   like cartoons.
              His fans
   anointed them "Picassos."
Compared to what he mastered
   in his "Blue Period," they seem
   at best a phase…
                Pearlstein's
   nudes appear exhausted.
The only feeling they arouse
   is sympathy…
             Egon Shiele
   and Gustav Klimt painted
   like "Peeping Toms."
             The yawning
   thighs of their nudes expose
   the hidden orifice of queens.
Drawn to perfection, they qualify
   as art.

Photographed, they'd be
pornography…
Compulsive over
cleanliness, Bonnard's wife
spent hours in a bath tub.
Her husband painted her there
time after time…
Rembrandt
painted Saskia in costume
or naked in bed.
Her expression
stayed the same in both.
Theories are a waste of time.
A woman attracts; a man
reacts.
Art as reaction
says less about the woman,
more about the man.

HELEN OF DUKE

We never met.
>> I knew you
> only through a book you mailed
> to me inscribed.
>> You wrote
> you married Bevington "just once…
> forever."
>> *A Book and a Love*
> *Affair* tells what that meant.
I learned you read to him
> (at his request) in hospice.
Afterward, you travelled:
> Spain, England, Crete, Kenya,
> France, Tibet, Egypt,
> Brazil, Peru.
>> You published
> travel diaries that read
> like Augustine's *Confessions*.
After your crippled son
> chose suicide, you travelled
> even more.
>> You came to know
> MacLeish by watching his eyes
> when he spoke, pronounced Reagan's
> optimism nothing but an act
> and joked with cummings over drinks.
When William Carlos Williams
> told you that girls found him

handsomer at sixty than he was
at twenty, you said, "Do you
want to bet?'
              The chore of travel
lessened to a bore.
                    You ran out
of destinations.
                You found
television a two-dimensional
fake of a three-dimensional
world.
        It lost in depth
what it gained in length and width.
After your mother died,
you wrote, "A better life
is better than death."
                Time
past returned as time present,
and your longest journey became
the distance from midnight to morning.

                    To Helen Bevington

THE FATE OF NOTHING

"The Devil's first trick is his Incognito."
—Denis de Rougemont

Forget the pitchfork, the red
    pajamas and the Satan sideshow.
Save those for Halloween.
What's diabolical reflects
    deficiency.
                    When we lack
    courage, the lack is devilish.
If we lack love and let it
    molder into hate, the lack
    is devilish.
                    When Omar Khayyam
    said, "I myself am heaven
    and hell," he meant that God
    and fate existed within him.
It's always been like that.
If we resist, we keep
    the devil at bay.
                    If we
    succumb, the devil has
    his way with us.
                    In case
    you've forgotten, the word *evil*
    hides within the word
    devil.
                    It's more than symbolic.
It's literally true and shows

what's mocked us since the world
began.
        Where some see losses,
others see gains.
             Where others
see pleasure, some see pain.
No matter what we see or do,
we're never certain in advance
if what we do is right,
or what we see is true.
What else explains why Abel
noticed nothing in his brother
to suggest his killer would be Cain?
By then it was too late
for anything but hate.
            And fate.

Responses

Trying to define a peninsula,
    one historian settled for
    "almost nearly an island."
Somehow that sounded better
    than the usual…
                        Asked
    how he felt during bouts
    of diarrhea, the boy answered,
    "Like I was sitting on an arrow…"
Ordered to retire after
    having spared his superiors
    the scandal they deserved, he had
    no option but silence.
                     His ongoing
    penance was to pray daily
    for the Jesuit order…
                      Informed
    that his Renault was totaled,
    he heard the medic ask him
    how he felt.
               "Malheureusement bien."
Injured or not, the French
    give irony its due…
Ever the envier, Iago called
    the total embrace of lovers
    "the beast with two backs."
The lovers ignored and pitied him…
"Rhetoric," said Yeats, "is the will

trying to do the work
of the imagination."
                    "Don't send
a poem," John Ciardi warned,
"on a prose errand."
                    "Cruelty,"
noted Thornton Wilder,
"is a failure of the imagination."
All three were speaking differently
    alike…
            Wounded by dementia,
    a retired linebacker said,
    "Anyone who plays for pay
    is earning profit for the owners."
Then he said it again
    because he forgot he'd said it…
Informed that Cardinal Ottaviani
    opposed his reforms, Pope John
    countered, "If he is telling
    the truth, we should listen."
Ottaviani said nothing more…
Invited to the States after
    receiving the Nobel Prize,
    Wislawa Szymborska politely
    responded, "Madam Szymborska
    will come when she is younger."

"WOULD YOU LIKE TO SEE WHERE JAMES JOYCE IS DEAD?"

The man who made the offer
  owned a Zurich Verlag
  that published Swiss authors
  in English.
          We taxied together
  to Fluntern Cemetery and walked
  where Joyce, Nora and son Georgio
  are buried near an embedded
  plaque beside a statue
  of Joyce.
          He looks less Irish
  than Swiss or French.
          Totally
  relaxed, he's seated in shirtsleeves
  with a cane slanted beside
  his crossed legs.
          A half-smoked
  cigarette slots between
  his cocked fingers…
          Campaigns
  to re-bury Joyce in Ireland
  clearly contradict his chosen
  exile from an Ireland that was.
Buried near him is Nobel
  Awardee Elias Canetti.
More tourists come for Joyce
  than Canetti.

Excepting *Dubliners*,
a masterpiece, Canetti for me
seems wiser, even in translation.

EPITAPH

Canetti was correct..
                    We write
    falsely of death because
    we "lack experience."
                    If truth
    is known only in retrospect,
    then death's unknowable because
    the dead are mute.
                    Meanwhile
    closure changes into myth.
Lives once taken live on
    after they end because
    they never end.
                    Is suffering
    the price we pay for finding
    happiness or simply the sadness
    of gratitude?
                    Death has no mercy,
    and hope is a gift.
                    As for
    an afterlife?
                    Resting
    in peace is death re-born
    as a nap to calm the immature.

Unseen at Sight

Sculptures of men in robes
    or uniforms or mounted on horses
    appear defiantly triumphant.
Sprinkled with droppings, they're still
    commanding.
            King Zeus keeps
    aiming his spear.
            Rodin's
    Balzac scowls while Dreyfus
    grips the broken sword
    of his injustice like a cross…
 Sculpted nude, the bodies
    of women command in silence.
No crowns or robes.
            No uniforms.
No horses.
       Forever in their prime,
    they wait in stone.
            They know
    their breasts and thighs are whispers
    destined to be overheard.
No longer hidden by clothes,
    they let their bodies speak
    without a gesture or a word.

INCOGNITO

You knew what it would mean
   to me before you helped
   to make it happen.
                  After
   it came without a card
   or signature, you acted surprised.
I asked if there was someone
   I should thank.
                 You said
   the giver would have signed
   the card if thanks were
   expected.
            Since then I've learned
   that gratitude lasts longer
   than acknowledgement.
                 You're just
   the opposite.
            You're pleased the most
   when those you love are pleased…
At family gatherings you capture us
   on camera.
           If not for you,
   the way we think we look
   would be as brief as memories.
The only one who's missing
   from a past your photographs
   preserve for us is you.

BY CHANCE

It seems too minor to mention—
    the day a Frenchman found
    my car-keys in Provence and refused
    a tip.
            "Pour la France," he said
    and smiled…
                   Or how my son
    at seven braved the bees
    to bring me Windex to defend
    myself against them.
                   My thanks?
"Get back inside right now…"
Or Monk who saved his nephew's
    life by giving him his kidney.
"I just need one," he said…
Or how Mary's adopted
    daughter from St. Petersburg
    starred in high school soccer
    and never talked of Russia…
What happens without notice
    or acclaim reminds me how
    a ship that's spotted by a man
    marooned for years but saved
    can almost civilize the sea.

UNFORESEEABLE

For Hatts, long gone, whose son
  in his sixties murdered twice.
For Cheryl, who emailed me
  at ninety because she wanted to.
For May, who faked compliments
  as coyly as she faked condolences.
For Frank, who taught his last class
  without knowing it would be.
For Grace, who said that women
  look older at fifty than men.
For Arthur Miller, who wrote
  America's best play so far.
For Judy, whose voice at seventy
  sounded better than at thirty.
For Anna, who never thought
  she'd have to until she had to.
For Selma, who knew what he was
  but married him anyway.
For Hamed, who asked why we make
  a sport of violence and collision.
For Maura, who wrote a book
  on what women know they know.
For Jean, who claimed that foresight
  at best was hindsight in reverse.
For Fred, who tamed his temper
  by swearing in sign language.
For me, who said we live
  in space but die on time.

With Nothing in Common Except

You learned best from travel.
I learned best by coming
home.
You never missed
anyone's birthday.
I had
to be reminded.
You planned
for possibilities.
I planned
for nothing but the time
being.
You always thought
of others first.
I had
to train myself to do it.
Gossips and braggarts bored you.
You showed me how to ignore them.
I never learned why
you liked beets or loved
rhythm more than melody.
No poet but me impressed you
but not that often.
Beyond
politics we favored Kennedy
because he never forced
a smile.

        All who followed him
faked it.
        We disagreed at times
but never mortally.
                For decades
we shared irrelevant differences
to learn that love made
all the difference.
                The rest
was trivia—nothing but trivia.

$E=MC^2$

I think of Luther, Rosa
    Parks, St. Joan of Arc
    and Albert Einstein.
                  Could
    Luther have assumed that saying
    "I can do no more" would launch
    the Reformation?
                 Did Rosa
    Parks foresee that keeping
    her seat in the front of the bus
    would change the South forever?
Who could predict that Joan
    of Arc would rise as the soul
    of France after being cursed
    and burned alive?
               And Albert
    Einstein?
             His perfect equation
    of energy, mass and light
    has nuclearized the world.
The formula is small enough
    to cover with a postage stamp.

THE GOSPEL ACCORDING TO

Unless we feel, we fail
  to remember.
            Those killed in war
  become just names or numbers.
And those who took their lives
  by choice?
            Additional numbers.
Or those who took the paths
  of least resistance?
            More numbers.
If we believe Erasmus,
  the world is ruled by folly.
What passes for honor is folly.
Statues commemorate the least
  noble.
            The infamous and wealthy
  are known eternally by name.
Assassins and saints are buried
  alike in cemeteries groomed
  like gardens.
            The folly of faith
  without love or action sullies
  what passes for religion.
            Entrepreneurs
  and men of state confirm
  Erasmus as a prophet...
            It takes
  a rebel, often a woman,

to choose the option of fools
and live for others.
                    By feeling
what she means and loving how
she lives, she cares for what
is overlooked or lost
and makes what's lasting last.

                    To Janine Bayer

V. AGAINST UNCERTAINTY

THE ODDS

We want what's intimate to last
    as surely as we want the life
    of touch, taste, sight, scent and sound
    to last forever.
              "Tomorrow
    I'll be here no longer," Nostradamus
    whispered when he died.
Fontenelle near death described
    his fear "…as nothing more
    than trying to go on living."
Dying of fever, Hopkins
    repeated, "I am so happy."
Reactions differ.
            Beliefs
    belie believers.
            All
    that lasts are chosen loves
    and what we hope is hope
    to wage against uncertainty.

Lightning Source UK Ltd.
Milton Keynes UK
UKHW051445091220
374661UK00027B/865/J

9 781951 319991